NIGHT

NIGHT

Etel Adnan

Nightboat Books
New York

© 2016 by Etel Adnan
Printed in the United States
Second Printing, 2017

ISBN 978-1-937658-53-3

An excerpt of *Night* was published in *A Public Space.*

Design and typesetting by Margaret Tedesco
Text set in Avant Garde Gothic and Berkeley

Cover/interior art, Colter Jacobsen: *Peace an accidental breathing space
(Coma)*, 2013, (detail). Magnifying glass, sun, record sleeve,
and giclée negative print. Diptych, 32 × 63 cm, (overall).
Courtesy of the artist and Corvi-Mora, London.

Cataloging-in-publication data is available
from the Library of Congress

Distributed by University Press of New England
One Court Street
Lebanon, NH 03766
www.upne.com

Nightboat Books
New York
www.nightboat.org

For Eugénie Paultre

It's always night,
otherwise we wouldn't need
light

—Thelonious Monk

Standing trees sleep in this forest that created the night when the moon was looking elsewhere. Gone the sailboats, the sea, in this obscurity that's keeping no promise

A field of rosebushes has been flattened by the wind.

Shadows strangely resemble yesterday's trees, yesterdays and tomorrows being the walls of our prisons.

Those shadows have landed us into taxis and houses, telling the light to stay outside

but the moon was right not to bother.

The wedding of history with the coffee we drink in our ever shrinking days awakes our need to reinvent love.

Empty shells lie on the beach in hours always uncertain.

The Indian will not cut the grass because, he says, that's his mother's hair, and I assured him that I will not break a stone because that might well be his spirit's house.

Philosophy brings us back to simplicity.

● ◗ ○

Now waves of roses are blanketing memory, but childhood's
desire to enter time's core remains. Nothing is stirring. Grass
grows differently than words. In those roses, infinity's infinity.

The wish to inhabit storms leads to cities in flames. Traces
turn into signs and thinking precedes itself in the deep
recesses of the brain. Bodies are always naked under their
clothes.

Words melt in reflections; that's why there's a uselessness to
this night, to my missing the river, to the delaying of love...
light is picking up momentum in the vicinity of the oaks that
cover this property, this silence.

Not to be able to climb up a mountain, run from this place to
the next, see things improving for friends or nations, or even
desire a clear day, not to stop the torture...

but this late afternoon, the fallen leaves were soft, walking on
them didn't seem to hurt any, they were friendly. I went a long
way. What happened later was of no importance.

Born in a sealed womb, where night is origin, I will say that something always remains from anything, even from nothingness.

Bitter bitterness. Thoughts worming in, as we move on smooth surfaces, though derailed here and there, or swim against the current, see the brain create lines of strawberries, banks of whales, angels, in profusion...

The world came into being, and didn't ask for maintenance; was it then pure mind? Those early hours still resonate as an echo, a breeze under the apple-trees. There was no need to rebel.

The deer, at this moment, is capering all over the fields.

Eternity is non evident. There's this endless rotation of the sun in the skull, the stillness outside, and a storm within. At least a river is always flowing in some part of the country. Winds, always gathering speed, shatter the order of things. We return home, in tears.

We leave for wherever History takes us. Preceded. Followed.

I peeled every trace of light off the walls. Withdrew into blurred definitions.

Today is a beautiful day. The gods are drunk, and the girls staggering with exhaustion. It's time to gather the poppies spread around, wave to the boats born so happy.

● ◗ ○

Yes, Tamalpaïs starts at the center. I recently climbed it, reached a soft spot and laid down. There was friendliness. As the sun was setting I moved up again. Suddenly, it was dark. The stars appeared, one by one. My capacities to think started to sink, making room for a strange contentment. Besides the many things they are, mountains are a language, probably the one most familiar to me.

● ◗ ○

When facing a mirror, a head resembles a lit planet. I wonder: can one spend time within a flower? Imagination moves in circles, as a sole piece of luggage on the tarmac.

With each bird flying, time is passing.

Night is an exhalation rising from a darkness foreign to it: a long eclipse.

I entered once someone's memory, I say through his brain, the seat of his illuminations. The place was planted with olive trees, and mathematical equations. On one of the trees was hanging a Van Gogh painting. The ground of that house of memory had been once the bed of a river that had run through still another person's brain. All this constitutes my spirit.

In its will to protect the living from the maddening effect of a constant present, nature created memory. An escape. A rest. Everything I do is memory. Even everything I am.

Knowledge doesn't kill as surely as love. We spoke at lunch of a guy who had driven three women to suicide. He was smaller in size than any of them, and perverse enough to boast about his deeds.

Our mind has a border line with the universe, there, where we promenade, and where tragedy resides.

Within bits of time volcanic eruptions sprout, and fall. Of all the energies we breathe, it's best to follow the ones that spring out of dreams. This season is cold, as cold as my soul.

Memory, and time, both immaterial, are rivers with no banks, and constantly merging. Both escape our will, though we depend on them. Measured, but measured by whom or by what? The one is inside, the other, outside, or so it seems, but is that true? Time seems also buried deep in us, but where? Memory is right here, in the head, but it can exit, abandon that head, leave it behind, disappear. Memory, a sanctuary of infinite patience.

Is memory produced by us, or is it us? Our identity is very likely whatever our memory decides to retain. But let's not presume that memory is a storage room. It's not a tool for being able to think, it's thinking, before thinking. It also makes an (apparently) simple thing like crossing the room, possible. It's impossible to separate it from what it remembers.

We can admit that memory resurrects the dead, but these remain within their world, not ours'. The universe covers the whole, a warm blanket.

But this memory is the glue that keeps the universe as one: although immaterial, it makes being possible, it is being. If an idea didn't remember to think, it wouldn't be. If a chair wasn't there, it wouldn't be tomorrow. If I didn't remember that I am, I won't be. We can also say that the universe is itself the glue that keeps it going, therefore it is memory in action and in essence, in becoming and in being. Because it remembers itself, it exists. Because it exists, it remembers.

To see something is to remember it; otherwise there's no seeing.

Memory is intelligent. It's a knowledge seated neither in the senses, nor in the spirit, but in collective memory. It is communal, though deeply personal. Involved with the self, though autonomous. At war with death.

It helps us rampage through the old self, hang on the certitude that it has to be.

But what about the ocean's intensity that echoes our own, the fever in cold weather, the soul's descent? What about the weight of the angels' wings?

● ◗ ○

And the night is an island covered with snow, life, always in the present tense,

in the nonchalance of a stream.

● ▶ ○

In the other-world, where will I find lodging for the Indians, the Hiroshima people, the many, many never buried, and where Omar Khayyam, he the dust, covered with his own words?

● ▶ ○

Memory can fail us ... We then enter barrenness, we silence the mind's deserts; a few events may emerge, oh so very few!

There must be non-human memories from where our own surges, take us to the next thing.

Memory and theatre work in similar ways. Memory trespasses our limits. Some animals hear it... some structures own it. Theatre started with the Greek oracle. In Delphi. When the Pythia was uttering her sound, her cry, she was passing a message from one world to an other, so that it be stored in human memory, and the people were watching, and the event was becoming a representation.

Thus a remembered event is a return to a mystery. When that happened for the first time, in pre-ancestral times, the creature that witnessed it as a return to the past was shattered.

● ◗ ○

My memories form a forest with unstable boundaries.
This forest has entrances in Northern California, Lebanon, Brittany... It's a field of tall trees and strange spirits. The dead do not scare us, that's what's wrong—we have let go of the power of fear. Streams are running, yes, but who's going to tell me how to find a way in the territory I'm speaking of, and if I don't find it, what am I living for?

Reason and memory move together.

● ◗ ○

And night and memory mediate each other. We move in
them disoriented, for they often refuse to secure our vision.
Avaricious, whimsical, they release things bit by bit.

Yosemite Valley occupies the same mental space as a corn
muffin; does the Valley also occupy the same inner space, when
I am in it as when I am thinking of it?

● ❯ ○

I have hallucinations about roofs falling on whole families,
a car running over a child, a stray bullet hitting right into a
heart... Those events show glaringly that we are mere objects.
Nature has its unavoidable laws.

Light is blinding, is the enemy. Desiring desire: that's when
a body disintegrates, and contaminates every river it has ever
known.

Lines of trees lining a dry land form a line of pilgrimage.
There's a beyond-ness to words.

Nothing matters besides the little town's yearning to go to sea,
to never return.

A cool summer breeze is different from a winter's same temperature.

Night is a subtle rain, wetting body and soul.

● ◗ ○

The place that was is now non three-dimensional, and its softness makes it appear and disappear; vagueness makes the future conceivable.

The order of things is not the one of the first experience of them: memory sews together events that hadn't previously met. It reshuffles the past and makes us aware that it is doing so.

Then, what are we left with? With recurring near-images which through centuries helped people think that they have visited the realm of the dead.

● ◗ ○

There are roughly 100 billion stars in the Milky Way, the same number as for the neurons in our brain. We may have to travel 24 trillion miles to the first star outside our star system to find an object as complex as the one that is sitting on our shoulders.

● ◗ ○

Always a flower planted on this body made of layers of shadows.

All elements are stratified obscurity, while the mountains file off like clouds. Eye and spirit are immersed into each other. By stages, in the night's fiber, bodies become visionary.

Memory is within us and reaches out, sometimes missing the connection with reality, its neighbor, its substance.

Simply to read what Brandon Shimoda has written "So much more can be seen! Light imposes a limit, or reveals it. Fall in the desert is starry. The wind brings the ocean, for which the desert is the afterlife."

● ◗ ○

I wonder: where was life's birthplace? The seconds advance toward the snow, sound after sound, one thought at a time.

While I was driving through Paris' lightbulbs under a steady drizzle, on wet asphalt, California was surging at every turn, there was therefore no destination to be reached.

The roots of the eucalyptus go in deep earth, in peace. The night's regular beat brings news not too different from those of Caesar's times. Down the coastline there's always the sea.

Words trace their way to the ocean. From the ridge facing this house, signals take off, scaring us, but a large stride, a deep breath, restores tranquility. Down there a stream is running as predictably as daily bread. The need to rest our hands on things.

The wind has veered to the south and the moon is dipping into the clouds. The town is not sleeping yet.The world is therefore being renewed.

The night was clear, and the depth of the mountain's slopes awesome: rivers were growling down into the valleys.

The moon was there, oh yes, speaking her language. My neck was hurting following her journey. On a cliff made of translucent marble, voices had stopped. Then the season showed a pervasive fear within Being's texture.

Each day is a whole year.

● ◗ ○

Worlds are pursuing their odyssey. Over buttes and mesas Indians are listening to their old epic tales. Their eyes remain fixed on the sun's center, on its ancestral rituals.

We have to break the absolute into prisms that distort perception into refraction and destruction. But the absolute can reassemble the pieces it has generated into new patterns for the world to restore itself. Nevertheless, the buildings across the street remain imperturbable.

It spreads like ink, moves like a forest animal, slides as fever in the veins: there's savagery to this obscurity.

A disoriented goat is challenging the unknown, entering it, it says. The night is crowned with dreams. It's because of their mortality that things exist. In all seasons. In immortality's split seasons.

In this night, all nights. All the oceans in this brain. Life pushes leaves out of this branch. Who are you, and where, drifting with the continents...

And Dedalus left for the sky, but to join whom? Or what? Large bands of clouds mingle with my mind's routine... I'm left behind. There's no breathing space left in this room.

Just an atmospheric pressure. A few chairs, a table. The air's paleness... Fragments from the soul are shed on those planes, trains or cars that take us to new miseries.

There's a heart in this body, a pump. Winds are prevailing. The house is painted with white chalk...you feel that something is passing bay.

To look at the green leaves against the black trunks of the trees is similar to asking a question. Water is running on the windowpanes toward a passage through the passage that life is, branching out. Fingers fetch hurting points, press on the soul.

We seek scratches over the moon's face. Shadows are
abandoning the objects that projected them. Mind has its own
phases and the river that shapes the landscape runs according
to its own whims. Standing by is the weather.

Are the rockets shooting for the moon killing invisible animals
on their way?

With what are we going to replace those incursions into the
inner nights where the knowledge of the void is knowledge of
fullness?

I would like to reach a galaxy and record its sounds,
or register an atom's activity. I wonder: would then any
discovered world be radically different from the familiar ones?

Often, the spirit runs swiftly, carrying the memory of women
to whom existence had presented an unbearable sharpness.
All I can tell is that I was there.

But what is spirit if not this fusion of the senses with the mind
that's willing the next instant to happen.

I am lying on a bed, the window half-open. There's death in the street, which feels like saying goodbye, or going downstream.

A fire is burning softly, being held by oceans of clouds. We are watching a cosmic phenomenon that's elevating us far above our daily condition.

Coming, coming, and coming again, the tides repeat Nietzsche's recurring passion for Dionysus, sustain his vision of the eternal return of the heroic times. For now, it's the return and the return of the ocean repeating itself over itself, water on water, movement over movement, waves over waves, breathing following breathing, affirmation coming over affirmation.

Tides, yes, breathing, love being a tide coming, and receding, a pendular insanity, as impatient in its regularity as this gaze on the inbuilt instability of liquid metals.

● ❭ ○

Let's think: the sea is terrifying; of course, when its whole mass stands up and creates havoc with its waves, we run for shelter. But she's more treacherous than that; she calms down, and her being then unfolds fully, and whoever looks then at her long enough is mesmerized, is out of his own being, transmuted...

that person will rather drown in her than continue to face that attraction which keeps the universe being.

● ◗ ○

A passenger is boarding a ship. Let's live before dying.

At times, an appetite for death creates a withdrawal into the nature of heat, turns the world into a blur.

A woman mourns her dead lover while everything buckles under her sorrow's pressure. Her days are going to grow longer.

I can hear the night's pulse. Divine will circulates around its edges. A precocious summer lies on a granite wall. The ocean is my land.

Disastrous are disasters. Paradise is such a lonely place that we are doomed, anyway. But at the meeting point of its rivers the horizon is always enlarged, the imagination, unleashed.

In the courtyard, the sun is scribbling shadows on the fading roses. I'm spending hours waiting for the next hour.

Love creates sand-storms and loosens reality's building stones. Its feverish energy takes us into the heart of mountains. Sometimes, a frozen moon illuminates frozen fields.

There's so much life around me, and I will have to leave.

● ◗ ○

My breathing is a tide. Love doesn't die.

● ◗ ○

A body when dead will never warm ours, and the sea will never cry over it, and time will become its bride.

● ◗ ○

As the "I" is immaterial we're really nowhere.

Night deepens, and this is the question: Who's dreaming whom? A fault-line separates us from our share.

Obscurity is half-memory, half sensation.

My own rhythm: a winter ending, mountains dissolving, waters on the rise.

The heat went unnoticed. We didn't hear from the dead as the ocean's roar had covered their sound. Cézanne was right in thinking that nature is interior.

The king, and son of God, Gilgamesh, found a darkish fruit in dark waters, and in there discovered the amplitude of his mortality.

This time, it's Eurydice that, naked, and with burns on her skin, is singing in Inferno.

By truckloads, the dead are arriving; she doesn't see how to gather the remnants of Orpheus' body.

● ◗ ○

My skin is my frontier. Things happen under it that I call feelings and ideas, and whose place of origin I will never find ways to visit.

I find redemption in desire; no interruption, in Nature. As mirrors duplicate space, we can multiply the universe by using reflectors. It has been clear to me, today, that it's better to follow the trails of a canyon than run after one's life.

Horses impregnated my father's genes during the last days of a vanishing empire. I hear their hooves on the dust road that leads to my door.

Between the "I" and the "me" a rain of poisonous lilacs, and your body next to mine as a distant and forbidden sunken sun.

These were velvety times as you had returned from a long journey that had taken you into the mystery of your flesh. The hours were raining like autumn leaves.

The light had been snuffed off your days.

You were sleeping as if still on Earth.

● ◗ ○

Sept 8th, 2015—Souls of people long disappeared, though immaterial and probably themselves disappeared, do suddenly act on us—it's love's awesome power.

● ◗ ○

Last night, a stormy night, Hegel visited my sleep, and I heard him say, with a rhythmic voice, that "man is this night, this empty nothingness: a wealth of infinite representations, images, none of which meant to be present to his spirit, or to be absent. It's night that exists here, (he continued), the intimacy of nature, the Self in all its purity". He insisted in saying that "night forms just a circle around man's imaginary representations: here a bloody head surging forth, there a white face, always disappearing brutally. That's the night that we see (he told me) when we look a man in the eyes; we sink then in a night of terror, the night of the world is then facing us."

He left, and I was still sleeping. Then he returned, wearing a long and dark coat, and only his face was lit. He went on telling me that "the power to pull out of this night images, or to leave them fall back, is the very act of asserting oneself, of stating the consciousness of the inner self, of action, division... It is into that night, (he said), that Being withdrew, but it is also in that night that the movement of this power has equally been stated."

Yes, life is spirit.

● ◗ ○

Joanne Kyger Doug Powell Stacy Szymaszek Ammiel Alcalay Anne Waldman David Buuck Thom Donovan an alignment of planets ...

Water brings energy the way memory creates identity.

Facing Van Gogh's last days would ruin one's head.

With a single candle, in a state of stupor, Dionysus lights the whole sky. Rivers meet at different speeds at certain points, turning the landscape into an epiphany. One's life is one's home.

... And the FBI forbidding Charles Olson to go to such a

non-country as Iraq, and us, the non-this and the non-that, ready to welcome anything that presents itself, and weary of daylight better to drink the ocean.

The weather as misty as my soul.

The Maximus Poems: under turbulent skies lagoons ships and sails sailors gone waves pounding tempests and fish and the guy changing gears constantly to keep the fun going.

●) ○

night of sovereignty
night of ecstasy
night of proximity

●) ○

I am a night bird. I search in barely visible corners the pencils, erasers, and writing slates of my early years...

I continue to hug walls. This hour is tired of dealing with

ancestors. Many things are receding along with the seasons, and the sun has set, that was just there

I will pursue my flight...

● ◗ ○

It's not a matter of finding some ink, no, or looking for a piece of paper. The lake my imagination perceives has kept on its blessed face a shimmer of light. Rivers will run for as long as they have already done; it's wrong to think that we're loved.

The sunset's last rays are defined by a flight of birds

There's a sweetness in the air that calls for death's coming. I try to deny the latter's presence because the birds, my brothers, have asked me to.

It's all because life, too, these days, has started to talk, and made me believe that night is a divinity made of all the others, and that in its heart trees are growing whose nature is of a new reality.

Night is the overflow of Being.

●) ○

The moon has drawn down one or two curtains. A thin rain is interfering.

I measure my memory of things, but not memory itself, as the present is also overflowing.

We create reality by just being. This is also true for the owl who's right now dozing on a branch.

A tiger tamed is as insignificant as the people who are taking the escalator of this building. Anguish sunk in red wine reappears as sunset.

Down, in the valley, war is unfolding its logic; on the other side of the ranch the ocean is raising a tantrum.

My father was born the year the idea of the eternal return occurred to Nietzsche; probably the same day.

A tree is always courageous. By the way, we're just a window on the world.

We need a rose-bush on the balcony, and the telephone not to ring.

I lived exclusively by my own wits, this is why I am a river.

Death had no temperature when it used to touch your skin. The will is never chartered, matter is frustrated by its limitations.

I'm asking you to see me lie on the traces that your body has left on the bed, but the heat belongs to you within our souls.

It happened in years no one has still in mind
I didn't try to do anything more than that.

My own disappearance followed a cloud that found me sitting in a garden.

Tunnels reproduce the patterns of arteries. There's a worm in the heart that's feeding on its allowance and birds in the courtyard for whom history is of no importance, while it has crushed our lives.

One day, the sun will not rise at its hour, therefore that won't be a day. And without a day, there won't be a night either. In that, Revelation will have perfected itself.

● ◗ ○

At 20 I was living at the door of reality, but I did not enter. There was no one to enter with, either. By the time I decided to go in, rivers had flowed, trees had grown, the seasons had aged. Soon later, I have had the chance to die, and I let it go; reality had no more reason to be.

Like a ship, you can shipwreck against the night.

● ◗ ○

It was said that people mattered, which they did, and we lost their shine.

It was also said that God is light, so that nobody and nothing could see Him. But some did. Therefore He is not light.

He resides in night. There's an affinity between the functions of our brain and those of God. He is memory, and the brain is an agent borrowing that memory, and it functions in total darkness. Like everything divine.

What we mean by "God" is that He is night. Reality is night too. From the same night.

● ◗ ○

This morning there was
    light,
tomorrow morning there
    will be light,

but where is light?

Conversations with my soul

(II)

Dear soul,
  I'm telling you,
you live not in
         me,
but around,
  in a circle,
  a cloud

Sleep next to me,
  where no one
  does

don't make me wait, as
  we know so little about
  each other

The heat is rising, the one
    that targets young
        predators when on an
        outing

Why are we lonelier when
    together, wherever that
    be

Shall we then search for
    love's trembling
    fringe

or sit under a pyramid's
shade,
somewhere in Mexico,
the clouds,
oh the clouds!

Curtains fall on sleeping
women
draw lines on
the table...

stay with me,
a while,
in my misery,
my insanity

don't lift the fog from my mind,
language is produced
by fear,
a headline:
war.

Do not cry,
terror is a stranger,
here,
close by

is an uncommon
piece of land,
your territory

in which I encounter
crumbs
from my being

There's a pond in the
garden,
fish
swimming,
and us,
from a different planet

Spring is returning, a
new animal...

death doesn't bring
another life, though it is an ominous
voyage

Close the window,
　　keep the news inside

the persistent fever

Dear soul, we're alive for a
　　short while,
dead, for an infinity of
　　time

would immortality
　be simply the survival of
　memory?

but doesn't memory
　　so often die
　　　　ahead of its owner?

Dear soul,
   am I only because I have been?

Billy the Kid has a
   bullet in the head,
like the Iraqi boy
   that he shot,
      willfully

My father was wounded where
   Illion once stood. His spirit had
   died much before his body

Sometimes the sea catches fire

My soul, sorrow takes different
names; which one will you
give it tonight?

The sea and the horizon
are just making waves

but the horizon is moving
over the sea...

and the river, across
my eyes, is moving
faster

The afternoon is
   trying to sort out
   its threads

Ezra Pound is
   climbing a volcano,
      his thoughts, burning

and me hearing water running down,
   spreading into
      the living-room...

Dear soul, we
  will part,
me becoming thinner
  than dust,
you, vanishing into a strange
  openness

tonight, I
  have invited
  my shadow.

Etel Adnan was born in Beirut, Lebanon in 1925. She studied philosophy at the Sorbonne, U.C. Berkeley, and at Harvard, and taught at Dominican College in San Rafael, California, from 1958–1972. In 1972, she returned to Beirut and worked as cultural editor for two daily newspapers. Her novel *Sitt Marie-Rose*, published in Paris in 1977, won the France-Pays Arabes award and has been translated into more than ten languages. In 1977, Adnan re-established herself in California, making Sausalito her home, with frequent stays in Paris.

Adnan is the author of more than a dozen books in English, including *Journey to Mount Tamalpais* (1986) *The Arab Apocalypse* (1989), *In the Heart of the Heart of Another Country* (2005), and *Sea and Fog* (2012), winner of the Lambda Literary Award for Lesbian Poetry and the California Book Award for Poetry. *To look at the sea it to become what one is*, a two-volume collection of writing, was published in 2014, the same year she was awarded France's l'Ordre de Chevalier des Arts et Lettres. Many of her poems have been put to music by Tania Leon, Henry Treadgill, Gavin Bryars, Zad Moultaka, Annea Lockwood, and Bun Ching Lam. Her paintings have been widely exhibited, including *Documenta* 13, the 2014 Whitney Biennial, CCA Wattis Institute for Contemporary Arts, The New Museum, and Museum der Moderne Salzburg. Mathaf: Arab Museum of Modern Art mounted a retrospective of her work in 2014.

NIGHTBOAT BOOKS

Nightboat Books, a nonprofit organization, seeks to develop audiences for writers whose work resists convention and transcends boundaries. We publish books rich with poignancy, intelligence, and risk. Please visit our website, www. nightboat.org, to learn about our titles and how you can support our future publications.

The following individuals have supported the publication of this book. We thank them for their generosity and commitment to the mission of Nightboat Books:

Elizabeth Motika
Benjamin Taylor

In addition, this book has been made possible, in part, by grants from the National Endowment for the Arts and the New York State Council on the Arts Literature Program.